IN THE PRESENCE OF GOD

PRESENCE FOREVER

AF582087

LIAM WANGSA

Copyright © Liam Wangsa
All Rights Reserved.

This book has been self-published with all reasonable efforts taken to make the material error-free by the author. No part of this book shall be used, reproduced in any manner whatsoever without written permission from the author, except in the case of brief quotations embodied in critical articles and reviews.

The Author of this book is solely responsible and liable for its content including but not limited to the views, representations, descriptions, statements, information, opinions and references ["Content"]. The Content of this book shall not constitute or be construed or deemed to reflect the opinion or expression of the Publisher or Editor. Neither the Publisher nor Editor endorse or approve the Content of this book or guarantee the reliability, accuracy or completeness of the Content published herein and do not make any representations or warranties of any kind, express or implied, including but not limited to the implied warranties of merchantability, fitness for a particular purpose. The Publisher and Editor shall not be liable whatsoever for any errors, omissions, whether such errors or omissions result from negligence, accident, or any other cause or claims for loss or damages of any kind, including without limitation, indirect or consequential loss or damage arising out of use, inability to use, or about the reliability, accuracy or sufficiency of the information contained in this book.

Made with ♥ on the Notion Press Platform
www.notionpress.com

I dedicate this book to every soul on earth, wrapped in God's infinite love and care, and every heart that beats with love for Jesus. May the words within its pages be a gentle reminder of His presence, His love, and His acceptance of you, just as you are.

Contents

Foreword

I am privileged to read before everyone this small yet life transforming book by our dear brother Liam. There are few books that have led me to my knees as I read them, this surely was one of them. The author has very clearly explained the revelation of the presence of God, which I believe, if anyone who reads with an open heart and mind will surely encounter. This book has definitely shifted my mindset about the presence of God. The testimonies mentioned by the author inspires me to sit with the precious Holy Spirit more and to have more intimacy with Him. As I went through the book it reminded me of my initial encounter with the person of the Holy Spirit, His tangible manifestation and the walk with Him. Definitely it has stirred up my hunger for more of Him and without doubt I would highly recommend it to anyone who seeks the presence of God.

-Pastor Mudang Tubin

Preface

As I reflect on my personal journey of encountering the presence of God, I am compelled to share my story with the world. This book is a testament to the transformative power of God's presence, which I have experienced firsthand.

My purpose in writing this book is twofold. Firstly, I want to assure everyone that experiencing Jesus is not exclusive to a select few. As I have personally encountered Him, I firmly believe that everyone can experience Him in a real and tangible way.

Secondly, I want to convey that the presence of God is far more profound and mysterious than we can ever imagine. It transcends our human experiences, thoughts, and emotions. As I have delved into the presence of God, I have come to realise that it is a boundless ocean that cannot be fully grasped by human understanding.

Through the pages of this book, I invite you to join me on this journey of discovery, as I share my personal experiences and reflections on the presence of God. My hope is that this book will inspire and encourage you to seek a deeper connection with God, and to experience the transformative power of His presence in your own life.

Acknowledgements

I extend my heartfelt gratitude to:

God Almighty, for His unwavering presence and guidance that inspired this book.

I am forever grateful to my spiritual parents and mentor, Senior Pastor Shajet Thomas and Ngurang Nini Shajet, for their selfless investment in my spiritual growth. Their leadership and teachings have profoundly impacted my journey, revealing the true essence of Jesus and the life-changing power of the Holy Spirit.

My beloved brothers in Christ, Techi David, Rohit Thapa, Krishna kumar, Gollo Tajik, Kornal Soren, Anok Kamhua and my elder brother Wangsan wangsa for their unconditional support and encouragement for this book.

Everyone who has walked with me through this journey, providing wisdom, prayers, and encouragement.

May this book bless and inspire readers to deepen their relationship with God.

Introduction

In the depths of our souls, we yearn for connection, for meaning, and for the assurance that we are not alone. This universal longing is rooted in our innate desire for God's presence.

Exploring the Presence of God" is an invitation to experience the profound reality of God's companionship in every moment. Through personal testimonies, biblical reflections, and practical insights, this book guides you on a transformative journey to:

- Deepen your understanding of God's presence beyond physical sensations
- Strengthen your faith in His Word and character
- Seek Him in every moment
- Find comfort in His constant companionship

Join me as we explore the breathtaking beauty of God's presence, and discover how it can transform your life.

CHAPTER ONE

INFINITE PRESENCE

As I slowly opened my eyes, the darkness of my room enveloped me like a warm embrace. The silence was palpable, punctuated only by the soft sound of my own breathing. It was still early, the sun had yet to rise over the sleepy town of Khonsa.

I woke up early that morning in my hometown, Khonsa, Arunachal Pradesh, India. It was still dark outside, and my room was quiet. As I woke up early in the morning, I was on my bed. The entire town was filled with calmness. At that time I just remembered God and how much He means to me. I got up and knelt down. It was still dark, my family members were still sleeping. As I woke up, I felt an overwhelming urge to sit in the presence of God and worship Him.

I started singing softly, just to myself. It was a way for me to express my feelings and connect with God. As I sang, after a few moments I felt a sense of peace washing over me. It was like God was right there with me, listening to my prayers. I started feeling the Love of God so strongly at that moment that I couldn't stop myself from crying. The tears started rolling down and the only word that was coming out of my mouth was 'Thank you Lord, Thank you Lord, Thank you Lord for your Love.' Endless words I have to say, but before Him I've been wordless each day.

As I was sobbing, my little sister, who was sleeping next to my room, heard me crying. She directly came towards my room, calling me, maybe she thought I had a bad dream or nightmare. But as she entered the room, she understood what was going on and she went back.

In that moment, everything else faded away. All that mattered was my connection with God. I felt so loved and so at peace. It was an experience I'll never forget.

Infinite Presence

The presence of God is the most precious thing we can acknowledge in our life. It is also one of the most profound and life-transforming subjects explored in the Bible. Despite our sincerest efforts to grasp it, God's presence remains unfathomable, surpassing our finite imagination and human understanding.

Here I want to share my experiences and practical insights, I hope it will encourage you in your daily walk with the Lord.

You may have opened this book expecting profound revelations about God's presence or extraordinary encounters. Instead, I'll share basic yet transformative perspectives that can revolutionise your relationship with Him.

These basic principles might resonate as familiar reminders or fresh insights, either way, they have the potential to profoundly impact your spiritual journey. Often, grasping the magnitude of God's presence begins with embracing the smallest, most overlooked aspects.

Through these pages, I invite you to rediscover the beauty in the everyday moments, and may these shared experiences inspire a deeper connection with our loving Father.

As we seek to understand God's presence, we acknowledge its transformative power in our lives. This realisation fuels our desire to deepen our connection with Him. This profound truth has sparked my desire to delve deeper into understanding God's presence.

Many People worldwide experience God's presence, yet each person's experience is uniquely personal. This diversity of experiences testifies to the boundless nature of God's presence. One day I was with one of my brothers, he shared a captivating insight that has stayed with me:

"He said, 'Liam, when we are with the Lord forever, we'll be astonished by the glorious nature and presence of God, with new and different wonders every moment. We will be experiencing his glorious presence and mighty things each moment, new and different.'

When He told me that, I was like, 'Wow,' but I could not

deeply understand what He really meant. The magnitude of His presence, the depth of His love, and the wonder of His glory were all still shrouded in mystery, waiting to be revealed in all their splendor. Yet, even in my limited understanding, I knew that I had caught a glimpse of something truly extraordinary.

I believe the beauty of God's presence is truly endless. It is something that cannot be fully understood or experienced, no matter how hard we try. And I think that is what makes it so amazing - we will be spending eternity uncovering the marvellous beauty that His presence holds.

As we journey through life and into the unknown, we will continue to discover new facets of His character, new expressions of His love, and new revelations of His majesty. It's like peeling back the layers of an onion - each moment reveals something more incredible.

Time and space will not be able to contain the beauty of His presence. We will be constantly amazed, constantly in awe. And even in eternity, we will still be exploring the depths of His love and beauty.

These things resonate deeply within me, fueling my longing to experience more of God's presence.

While there are various levels and dimensions of God's presence, this book focuses on a singular, in this book, I share about some of my experiences with the Lord and a pivotal lesson the Lord has personally taught me about His presence - a revelation that has changed my perspective. As I share these experiences and lessons with you, my prayer is that you will be inspired to seek a deeper encounter with God's presence in your own life.

CHAPTER TWO

WHEN JESUS BECAME REAL

Have you ever felt like you are missing something in your life, something that is hard to explain? For me, that feeling was like a nagging whisper in the back of my mind, a gentle reminder that there was more to life than what I was experiencing. I had tried to fill the void with all sorts of things - relationships, accomplishments, possessions but nothing seemed to satisfy the deep longing in my heart. It was not until I encountered the presence of God that I finally found what I had been searching for.

The presence of God is one of the most precious and marvellous experiences I have had in my walk with the Lord. At the age of 19, I encountered the precious Holy Spirit and experienced the presence of God in my life, and my life transformed in ways I never imagined.

I was born into a loving Christian family in Khonsa, a small town nestled in the heart of Arunachal Pradesh, India. Growing up in this devout household, Sunday services and gospel programs were an integral part of our family's spiritual routine, never to be missed. Every Sunday, without fail, my parents diligently sent me to Sunday school.

In Sunday school, I was surrounded by children who excelled in various areas some spoke fluent English, others effortlessly read the Bible, and many sang beautiful hymns. However, as a child, I often felt uncomfortable among them, struggling to keep up with their talents.

Despite my apprehensions, attending Sunday school was non-negotiable, as it was my parents' order. So, every Sunday, I would reluctantly join my peers, feeling a mix of emotions - from nervousness to curiosity. As a result, Sunday became the day I dreaded most for me, the worst day of the week.

Little did I know that these early experiences would shape my spiritual journey and lay the foundation for a deeper connection with God.

As I matured, my interest and activism in the Lord grew. I led worship in the Church and became one of the most engaged youths in the Church. Yet, my understanding of Jesus was very limited to what I heard from my family, pastors, elders and movies.

For a long time, Jesus was just a figure in my beliefs, not a living presence in my daily life. My understanding of Him was limited to the basics: He is God, He loves me, He died for my sins, He heals the sick, and He'll return one day. While these truths could lead me to salvation, *Jesus did not just want me to have his salvation, He wanted me to have him.*

more – a personal, intimate connection with me.

Jesus did not just sacrifice Himself for my forgiveness; He longed to be my constant companion, my guide, and my friend. The Bible beautifully captures this in ***John 15:13***, *"Greater love has no one than this, than to lay down one's life for his friends." He considers me His friend!*

As the Good Shepherd, Jesus laid down His life for His sheep – for me ***John 10:11.*** His love knows no bounds, and He desires a deep, meaningful relationship with me. ***Galatians 2:20*** reminds me, "He loved me and gave Himself for me.

Although I was blessed to be born into a devoted Christian family, where faith was a cornerstone of our daily lives, and grew up surrounded by the loving community of believers, I still lacked a profound personal connection with Jesus. I was one of the most active youths in my Church, I diligently attended every Sunday service, participated in numerous gospel programs, and engaged in various spiritual activities.

However, despite this fervent exterior, I surprisingly never experienced a genuine, heart-to-heart and person-to-person encounter with Jesus. My faith was rooted in tradition, family legacy, and religious routine, rather than a personal relationship with Him. I never had a moment where I felt His presence, heard His voice, or experienced His transformative power.

Growing up, I was constantly reminded of the importance of having a close relationship with Jesus. However, despite the countless sermons, teachings, and discussions, I never truly grasped the depth and significance of this relationship until I came to know the Holy Spirit.

Yet, the mercy of the Lord was upon me. He providentially led me to a godly mentor, who introduced me to the precious Holy Spirit who transformed my life totally.

At 19, I met Pastor Shajet Thomas(the founder of RBIM Revival Blessing International ministries) who later became my beloved father in the Lord. who taught me the true meaning of following Jesus Christ and introduced me to the precious Holy Spirit. This transformed my life forever, knowing the Holy Spirit was enough to change my life forever. Jesus became incredibly real to me; Christianity became meaningful. My desire to experience Him grew, leading to supernatural experiences.

As I reflect on my journey, I have come to a profound realisation: Jesus is not merely a beautiful narrative crafted by humanity, but the very One who transforms people's stories into breathtaking masterpieces. And the most astonishing truth is that He is just as real and present today as He was 2,000 years ago. *He is not a beautiful story made by men, He is a beautiful story maker of men.*

This truth sets my heart ablaze, fueling an insatiable desire to experience Him in my life. I declared, "If the Lord is truly real, and people are genuinely experiencing Him, then I want to experience Him too - no matter what it takes.

Every night, I started to pray, 'Lord, I want to experience you'. I became desperate to experience him, I tried to do anything I could do to experience him.

Outside my rented house, amidst swarms of mosquitoes, I found an unlikely sanctuary. During the Covid-19 pandemic, our church was forced to close due to government restrictions on physical gatherings. Determined to maintain fellowship, our church family shifted online, holding nightly meetings on Zoom.

I did not have my personal space to call my own. I had join these virtual gatherings outside my rented house, armed with a lamp to illuminate the darkness and mosquito killer spray to ward off the relentless insects. The outdoor area was infested with mosquitoes, making every meeting a test of endurance.

To minimise distractions, I had temporarily turned off my camera during the meeting to quickly spray any mosquito biting me. Yet I was resolute in my pursuit to know the Lord more and experience Him.

We were living in a small rented house with only two rooms and one kitchen. My parents occupied one room, while my brother and I shared the other room and bed.

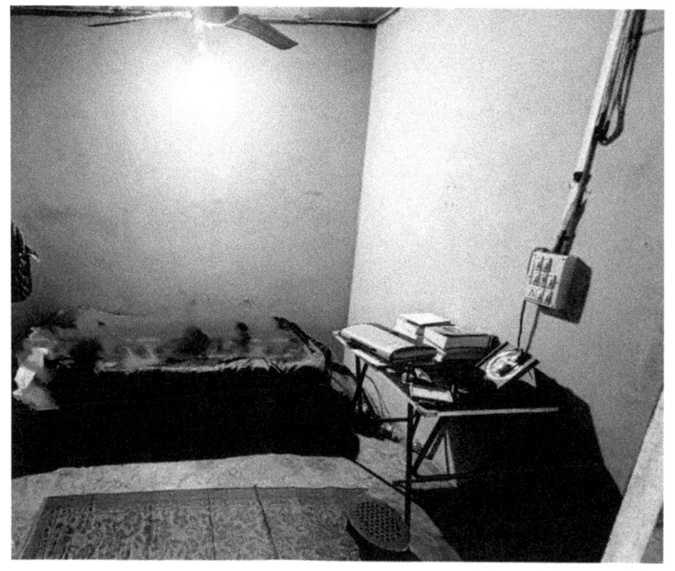

The room I shared with my elder brother

I had a personal prayer time every night alone in our kitchen, asking the Lord to experience Him. At first, I didn't feel anything, but I didn't give up.

Since I did not have a personal space, I waited for my family to fall asleep. It was then that I would quietly make my way to our kitchen. It was tiny, I couldn't even move around there, surrounded by buskets and a gas cylinder, yet every night, I would find myself drawn there to worship and I would pray every night,"Lord, I want to experience you."

The Kitchen where I prayed.

I yearned to experience Jesus with all of my heart, whom I had believed in since childhood, of whom I have heard for so long in my life, but never had a personal encounter. So, every night, after my family slept, I'd go to the kitchen to pray and worship.

Initially, the only sensations I experienced were the smell of gas and the occasional presence of rats and cockroaches scurrying by. Sometimes they would make a faint sound, and I would instinctively think, "It is Lord, maybe," and then, with a mix of hope and uncertainty, I would open my eyes, only to be met with the sight of those rats. Yet I wanted to experience the Lord. During those days, the only prayer I prayed for was, Lord, I want to experience you. Every night I would sit in the kitchen, and wait for His presence.

It was how I began my walk with the Lord from our small kitchen with rats and cockroaches. Yet the Lord is faithful, He never fails the desires of a heart that genuinely seeks Him, as the Bible says in ***Jeremiah** 29:13 And you will seek Me and find Me, when you search for Me with all your heart.*

In a moment that would forever change the trajectory of my life, something truly miraculous happened. Weeks of fervent prayer had led up to this instant, and then, it happened. I felt God's presence for the first time in my life. During the prayer, suddenly, my hands began to shake like a fan unstoppable, as if the heavy wave of winds had touched my hands. It was my first experience that will forever be etched into my soul. Following that encounter, I began to experience a deeper sense of His presence in my life, impacting every aspect of my daily routine. After that whenever I sit for prayer and worship most of the time I would experience His presence. Sometimes, I felt His presence strongly, like someone holding my hands. At such times, His Presence would permeate my being, inducing a physical response—a shiver, a tingle, a goosebumps rising on my skin. Other times, it was quieter, but I still knew He was with me.

My experiences with Jesus taught me that He is not just a distant figure; He is a real, and He is with me, my constant companion. We can talk and share our thoughts and feelings, like one sharing with his friend.

But it was not always tangible. There were moments when I simply felt the Lord's presence, sensing that someone was near me - and I knew, without a doubt, it was Him. His presence was unmistakable Looking back, I realise that experiencing Jesus was not a one-time thing; it's a lifelong journey. It's about listening to His gentle voice and feeling His presence in everyday moments.

When I had a personal encounter with Jesus, my life was completely transformed. I could not realise how much He had changed me. I was not someone who did not know about Jesus - I grew up in a Christian family, learned about the Bible, and was very active in the church. I thought I loved Jesus and knew everything about Him. Yet when I experienced Him personally I was like 'Lord, I want to know you more.

The experiences I was having were different. It was like nothing I had ever felt before in my life. I realised that being born into a Christian family or being active in church is not enough. What really matters is having personal encounters and fellowship with the Lord.

After these encounters, I felt like a completely different person. Exactly what the Bible means to be born again or a new man ***(2 Corinthians 5:17***).

I was not trying to change myself or do anything special. I was just spending time in his presence, a personal fellowship with Him. And that's when the transformation happened.

CHAPTER THREE

ETERNAL GLORY

I still remember the excitement and anticipation that filled my heart as the clock struck midnight on December 31st, 2021. It was a night like any other, yet it held a special significance for me and my fellow believers. As we gathered at our church for the watchnight service, I couldn't help but feel a sense of expectation, a sense that something special was about to unfold...

It was on 31st December 2021, a night that would forever be etched in my memory, during the watchnight service at our church. Our church was decorated with an array of beautiful lights and colours. All my brethren were looking beautiful that night, everyone was dressed in their best clothes, their faces radiant with joy and reverence as we all gathered to worship the Lord.

As the time ticked closer to midnight, the excitement in the air grew. Many people had come to attend the service, all eager to bid farewell to the old year and welcome the new one with hope and expectation. Our pastor, a vessel of the Lord, began to pray, and I, along with the brethren, knelt down in reverence.

As we prayed, I felt a sudden, wonderful Presence. It was as if the very atmosphere in the church had shifted, and we were enveloped in the glory of God. I heard the sound of weeping and wailing of those who were near me, as if their hearts were being poured out before the Lord. I believe my brethren had the same experience of His presence which I had at that moment. I clearly can still remember, for a moment we all cried in a loud voice, even as I'm writing this I could hear the voice of one of my brothers who was just near me.

The presence I felt was too marvellous, it was so wonderful that I cannot put it down into words. This moment was just for a couple of minutes yet it was so wonderful that I wanted to remain there forever, crying in His presence, basking in the radiance of His glory. I feel so dissatisfied as I'm writing this because I cannot find words that can adequately describe the glorious presence I experienced at that moment.

That day, I realised how the elders and angels in heaven are worshipping the Lord day and night without rest. As the Bible says, "***Revelation 4:8-10*** *The four living creatures, each having six wings, were full of eyes around and within. And they do not rest day or night, saying: "Holy, holy, holy, Lord God Almighty, Who was and is and is to come!" [9] Whenever the living creatures give glory and honour and thanks to Him who sits on the throne, who lives forever and ever, [10] the twenty-four elders fall down before Him who sits on the throne and worship Him who lives forever and ever, and cast their crowns before the throne, saying:*

I caught a glimpse of that heavenly worship that night, and it left me in awe of the majesty and glory of our God.

I firmly believe the elders and angels in heaven do not worship day and night without rest because of fear and mandate, but I believe they are not able to stop themselves from worshipping the Lord when they see or experience the glory of the Lord in heaven. They are completely enthralled by the majesty and splendour of God's presence, and they cannot help but pour out their hearts in worship and adoration. Their worship is not driven by obligation or duty, but by an unrelenting passion to honour and glorify the Lord. They are irrepressibly drawn to the throne of God, and their worship is a spontaneous and heartfelt response to the overwhelming beauty and glory of the Lord.

***Revelation 4:10-11**: The twenty-four elders fall down before Him who sits on the throne and worship Him who lives forever and ever, and cast their crowns before the throne, saying: [11] "You are worthy, O Lord, To receive glory and honour and power; For You created all things, And by Your will they exist and were created."*

I believe the worship should come from the depth of our being in awe of His glory. It should originate from the innermost part of our being, from the deepest recesses of our heart, soul, and spirit. It should be a response to the awe-inspiring glory of God. Worship should not be just about external actions, such as singing, praying, or attending church services, it should be our being responding to the glory of His nature that even we ourselves couldn't stop our being. This kind of worship is not something that

can be manufactured or forced, but rather it is a spontaneous and authentic response to the majesty and splendour of God's presence.

If this happens in churches today, I believe the entire world would experience the glory of the Lord. The presence of God would be palpable, and the power of His glory would be unleashed upon the earth. As the Bible says, *"For the earth shall be filled with the knowledge of the glory of the Lord, as the waters cover the sea"* (***Habakkuk 2:14***).

I believe this is the reason why we will be in awe of His glory and majesty for eternity. What a glorious God and a mighty God we serve! His majesty is beyond human comprehension, and His glory is so radiant that it will captivate our hearts and minds for all eternity. Hallelujah! Also the Bible says His glory is above the earth and heaven. ***Psalm 148:13*** *says, "Let them praise the name of the Lord, for his name alone is exalted; his glory is above the earth and heaven."*

Once I heard a servant of God said, "When we meet the Lord face to face I can assure you, when we meet the Lord Jesus face to face, you will forget your name, you will forget yourself, you will forget that you are a theologian, scholar, a church leader, a pope, a cardinal, I don't really care what kind of hierarchy, when you meet the Lord Jesus, His awesomeness, His beauty, His holiness, His perfection, His mightiness will blow you and everything with you away, you will be speechless." -Bishop MarMari Emanuel

1 Corinthians 13:12 AMP *[12] For now [in this time of imperfection] we see in a mirror dimly [a blurred reflection,* *a riddle, an enigma], but then [when the time of perfection comes we will see reality] face to face. Now I know in part [just in fragments], but then I will know fully, just as I have been fully known [by God].*

When we finally stand before Jesus, face to face, in all His glory, our identity of this world will disappear, denominational affiliations and ministry labels will fade into insignificance. The things that seem so important now will fade away. We'll see that our arguments over minor differences were a waste of time.

And yet, it's ironic that in our present-day pursuit of faith, many of us find ourselves entangled in debates over doctrine and denominational loyalty. We forget that the kingdom of God is not about our denominational identity, but about the transformative power of Jesus Christ. As the Bible says, *'For the kingdom of God is not a matter of talk but of power.'* ***I Corinthians 4:20 NIV***

I firmly believe that those who have genuinely encountered the radiant beauty and glory of God's presence will not be sidetracked by these earthly concerns. Instead, they will be captivated by a singular passion: to reflect the breathtaking beauty of Jesus to a world.

Their hearts will beat with a desire to demonstrate the compassion, kindness, and generosity of Christ to a world that is crying out for hope. They will be driven by a burning desire to share the Good News of the Gospel with those who are lost, broken, and searching for meaning. And as they do, they will find that the petty distinctions and divisions that once seemed so important will fade into insignificance, replaced by a deep and abiding sense of unity and purpose in Christ.

CHAPTER FOUR

THE PRESENCE OF GOD

The carefree days of my youth, when the thrill of adventure beckoned me to explore the world beyond my doorstep. I was a boy who loved to wander, to roam with my friends. Not a single day would pass without me going out with my friends.

But as the seasons of my life began to change, so too did my priorities. I found myself drawn to a new pursuit, one that brought me a sense of purpose and fulfilment that I had never known before. I began to crave time with the Lord, to sit at His feet.

And so, when my friends would call me to join them on their adventures, I would lie to them, telling them that I had important work or family obligations that I could not ignore. It was not that I did not value our friendships. But now, my desire was changed, my passion was changed, and I felt an insatiable hunger to pursue a new path, one that was calling to me with an irresistible voice.

The tapestry of my life has undergone a profound transformation, woven with threads of change and renewal. Like a river that has altered its course, I have been redirected, flowing in a new direction that is both unexpected and exhilarating. I no longer frequent the places that once held my attention, nor do I engage in the activities that previously brought me joy. The things that once thrilled me now lie dormant, as my desires and the trajectory of my life have shifted in a direction I never could have anticipated.

Now Jesus became so real to me, his presence became so real in my life that I could experience it, I started having daily personal time with him. The presence of the Lord became incredibly precious to me, leading me to prioritise our time together. I began distancing myself from friends I once spent entire days with, now eager to spend hours with Him instead. When visitors came to my home, I found myself awaiting their departure, anxious to return to my time with the Lord I vividly remember a moment when I was with God in my room. I was praying and worshipping Him, and His presence enveloped me. It was a precious time of intimacy with the Lord.

But then, my parents interrupted my quiet time, asking me to run an errand. I obediently left my room, feeling a sense of disconnection from God's presence.

As I rode my scooty to complete the task, I expressed my longing to God on the way, 'Lord, it was so good in the room, but now I do not feel Your presence. What I can feel now is the noise of vehicles, people in the market.

My heart longs to experience His presence daily, but it seems impossible amidst worldly responsibilities and duties.

I have long wrestled with a burning question, posing it to the Lord and many others, yet the responses never fully resonated with my soul. Until, in a profound moment, the Lord chose to answer me directly, imparting a revelation that brought peace and understanding and changed my perspective.

The question I had which I eagerly wanted to know was "Can I be in God's presence all the days of my life"? At first, I thought it would be amazing to always feel His presence, to walk in the light of His love and guidance constantly and everyday. But my understanding of the presence of God was limited, confined to moments of intense spiritual experience. I thought God's presence was only felt during prayer and worship in the room or Church, through physical sensations like electric vibrations and shaking of hands, feeling cold and warm, etc.

Early in my walk with God, I deeply desired to feel His presence daily, just like during prayer and worship. Having never encountered anything comparable in the world before, I asked God, 'can I stay in your presence all the days of my life? Is it possible to be in your presence all the time without break? But how? I cannot be in my room praying all the days of my life, I have college, I have to be with my family, friends, and ministry works.' I wondered how I could be in the presence of God all the time.

I longed to experience God's presence consistently, beyond just moments of prayer and worship in the room and Church services. I wanted to know if it was possible to maintain this intimate connection in every aspect of my life." Because the presence of God I was experiencing was too marvellous for me and I desire to be in his presence all the days of my life.

At that moment, I thought experiencing God's presence required a quiet, personal setting. Yet, a question lingered within me; I asked myself and the Lord, 'Is it possible to be with You all the time every day, Lord?' I yearned for a continuous connection with God beyond isolated moments.

However, my limited understanding led me to conclude, 'It's only possible if the whole world disappears, and I am alone with You.' I struggled to imagine maintaining a constant connection with God amidst life's distractions.

I yearned to stay in God's presence throughout the day. How could I maintain this connection amidst daily activities like going to college, visiting markets, and attending events, family and friends? How could I keep my focus on Him while navigating life's challenges? God taught me a valuable lesson, though it was not always easy. He gently revealed the depths of His presence, encouraging me to seek Him in every moment.

Previously, I felt God's presence through tangible sensations that brought me comfort, peace, and joy. I had supernatural experiences in my room many times during prayer and worship, where I felt His loving embrace, guidance, and reassurance.

But there were moments of days, when those experiences and feelings have faded away, leaving me with a deep sense of longing. I no longer sense the Lord's presence as I once did, and I have begun to doubt myself, wondering if I've done something wrong or mistake.

Have I neglected prayer and worship? Did I fail to study God's Word daily? Is this due to some sin or mistake?' I asked myself, searching for answers. The more I questioned, the more uncertain I became.

The loss felt suffocating, like someone had stolen my breath or a part of my being. It was as if I had lost my anchor. Every day felt empty, devoid of purpose.

Desperate for answers, I cried out to the Lord, pouring out my heart in prayer. But the silence was deafening, leaving me discouraged and defeated. I felt lost, unsure how to regain that intimate connection.

One remarkable day, amidst my discouragement, the Lord spoke directly to my heart. His gentle whisper pierced through my doubts and fears. He said, "You believe that I am with you when you feel Me, or experience me. But I am with you always, regardless of your emotions and feelings. I am with you not only in your room when you feel but always even when you don't feel me."

That day I realised, the Lord wants me to know him beyond my experiences and feelings, His presence in my life is beyond my experiences and emotions.

In that moment, a profound revelation dawned on me. God desires us to experience Him deeply, but not limit Him to those moments. He wants us to trust His promises, to stand firm on His Word, and find stability in His unchanging character.

This truth transformed my perspective, shifting my focus from fleeting emotions to eternal truth. I realised that my relationship with God was not solely dependent on tangible sensations or supernatural experiences.

Rather, it was built on the rock-solid foundation of His Word, promising:

"I will never leave you nor forsake you." **(Hebrews 13:5)**

"I *am with you always, even to the end of the age."* ***(Matthew 28:20)***

"You will seek Me and find Me when you seek Me with all your heart." ***(Jeremiah 29:13)***

These promises became my anchor, holding me secure through life's turmoil.

With renewed conviction, I began to delve deeper into Scripture, discovering the richness of God's character, His love, and His faithfulness.

This shift from emotional experiences to biblical truth brought freedom and stability to my walk with God. I learned to trust His promises, even when my feelings fluctuate.

Now, I see that God's presence is not limited to moments of intense emotion; it's a constant, unwavering reality, rooted in His unchanging Word.

But it does not mean that just knowing He is with you all the time, you stop spending secret time with Him or lose desire to experience His presence. Quite the opposite, when you grasp His promises and Word, confirming He is always with you, it ignites a deeper longing to dwell with Him. You will desire to cultivate a more intimate relationship, seeking moments of quiet contemplation and communion.

This understanding fuels your passion to:

-Spend quality time in prayer and worship
-Dive deeper into Scripture, uncovering -hidden treasures
-Seek His guidance and wisdom in every decision

You will crave more of His presence, hungry for the nourishment only He provides.

In fact, knowing He is always with you becomes the foundation for a more vibrant, dynamic relationship. You'll want to:

-Share your thoughts, emotions, and -dreams with Him
-Listen for His gentle whispers and guidance -Explore the depths of His love and character.

Sometimes, God intentionally remains silent to help us grow in understanding His presence. He wants us to know Him because of our faith, not just feelings, as the Bible says ***Hebrews 11:6*** *But without faith it is impossible to please Him, for he who comes to God must believe that He is, and that He is a rewarder of those who diligently seek Him.*

This silence can be challenging, but it's an opportunity to deepen our roots in Christ. It's a call to seek Him with all our heart, to meditate on His Word day and night. This understanding has given me courage to persevere.

I stopped relying on physical sensations and began declaring, 'Thank you, Lord, for being with me always. I know you are here.' I meditated on His presence, teaching my consciousness to acknowledge His constant companionship. I began to see God's hand in every detail, every conversation, every challenge. His presence became my comfort, my peace.

The presence of God is not just physical vibrations or shaking hands; it is really knowing the person of God that is with us. ***We do not lack his presence, we are not just aware of it always.***

I remember an incident in the Bible when Nathaniel was under the fig tree. He did not know about Jesus but Jesus said He saw him even before Philip called him. ***John 1:45-48 NKJV Philip found Nathanael and said to him, "We have found Him of whom Moses in the law, and also the prophets, wrote—Jesus of Nazareth, the son of Joseph." [46] And Nathanael said to him, "Can anything good come out of Nazareth?" Philip said to him, "Come and see." [47] Jesus saw Nathanael coming toward Him, and said of him, "Behold, an Israelite indeed, in whom is no deceit!" [48] Nathanael said to Him, "How do You know me?" Jesus answered and said to him, "Before Philip called you, when you were under the fig tree, I saw you."***

Jesus was watching over me even when I did not know about Him. God's presence is not confined to emotions; it's rooted in scriptural truth. His Word is our rock, our foundation. It's the anchor that keeps us grounded in life's turbulent sea.

CHAPTER FIVE

GOD IS AS CLOSE AS YOUR NEXT HEARTBEAT

For a day in Your courts is better than a thousand. I would rather be a doorkeeper in the house of my God Than dwell in the tents of wickedness. ***-Psalms 84-10***

Imagine being loved without condition, pursued with passion, and welcomed with open arms. This is the heartbeat of God, a love that defies human understanding and transforms our lives forever. It's a love that sees beyond our flaws and failures, our doubts and fears, and yet chooses to pursue us with unrelenting passion. A love that whispers our name in the darkest moments, and celebrates our triumphs with unbridled joy. This is the love of God, and it's a love that can change everything. ***Jeremiah 31:3*** *The Lord has appeared of old to me, saying: "Yes, I have loved you with an everlasting love; Therefore with lovingkindness I have drawn you.*

The most beautiful thing about God's presence I have discovered is that the Lord wants me to be in His presence more than I want to be in his presence. This truth has transformed my understanding of His love and desire for intimacy.

Regardless of who you are or what you have done, Jesus wants to be with you; He wants you by His side ***(John 17:24).*** This unconditional love is staggering, especially when we consider our own limitations and failures. It's a love that is not based on our merits or achievements, but rather on His own inherent nature as a loving Father.

The Bible says, "For God so loved the world that He gave His only Son" (***John 3:16***). This verse reveals the depth of God's love; He did not wait for us to seek Him, but instead, He initiated the relationship. It's not "the world so loved God that they sought Him," but rather "God so loved the world that He came down to them" (***Philippians 2:5-8***). This verse highlights God's proactive pursuit of humanity.

Once a servant of God said, "*God proved His love on the Cross. When Christ hung, and bled, and died, it was God saying to the world, 'I love you.'" ~ Billy Graham*

Jesus declared, "I came to seek and save the lost" (***Luke 19:10***). He desires to be with each of us, regardless of our past or present circumstances.

God's Word reassures us, "The Lord is near to all who call upon Him, to all who call upon Him in truth" (***Psalm 145:18***). His presence is accessible, and His love is unwavering.

In ***Romans 8:38-39***, *Paul writes, "For I am convinced that neither death nor life, neither angels nor demons, neither the present nor the future, nor any powers, neither height nor depth, nor anything else in all creation, will be able to separate us from the love of God that is in Christ Jesus our Lord."* I firmly believe Paul penned these words when he discovered the vastness of God's love for us, not when he discovered his own love for God. This distinction is crucial.

Paul's revelation was not about his own devotion or efforts to love God, but about the unwavering, unrelenting love God has for humanity.

When we delve into **Romans 8**, starting from **verse 31**, we witness Paul's unwavering boldness and confidence. But what fuels this confidence? It's not his own love for God, but God's love for us.

Romans 8:31 asks rhetorically, "What then shall we say to these things? If God is for us, who can be against us?" Paul's emphasis is on God's stance towards us, not our stance towards Him.

In Romans 8:37, he declares, "Yet in all these things we are more than conquerors through Him who loved us." Notice the phrase "through Him who loved us," not "through us who loved Him." This subtle distinction underscores Paul's message:

It's not about our love for God; it's about His love for us.

I John 4:10 *In this is love, not that we loved God, but that He loved us and sent His Son to be the propitiation for our sins.*

Paul's boldness stems from recognizing God's unwavering support and affection. He is not boasting in his own devotion, but revelling in God's unrelenting love.

This perspective shift transforms our relationship with God:

-From performance-based to gift-based
-From earning love to receiving love -From self-effort to divine empowerment Paul's confidence inspires us to:
-Trust God's goodness, regardless of circumstances
-Rest in His love, not our own efforts
-Face challenges with courage, knowing God's for us.

God loves us to be with him more than we do. He loves you more than you love him.

I read a powerful book called **'Good Morning Holy Spirit'** by Pastor Benny Hinn, one of the most precious books I've come across. In the book, Pastor Benny Hinn shared his wonderful experience with the Holy spirit:

"One evening, as I was about to leave my room, I felt the presence of the Holy Spirit. I saw Him standing before me, and I knew I was not alone.

As I turned to leave, I heard the gentlest voice whisper, "Benny, don't go."

I turned back, and the Holy Spirit asked, "Will you stay with Me for a while?" I was deeply moved and humbled. "Lord, I'll stay with You forever," I replied."

That moment taught him (and us) the value of:

-Spending quality time with the Holy Spirit

- Listening to His gentle whispers
- Yielding to His guidance and transformation

God loves us to be with him more than we do. Once a servant of God said, "*God wants us so badly that he has made the condition as simple as he possibly could: Only believe.*"
~ Smith Wigglesworth
God's love precedes our love for Him ***(1 John 4:19).***

*His love is not based on our merits or actions (****Romans 5:8****). Nothing can sever us from His love* ***(Romans 8:38-39****).*

This promise reminds us that nothing can separate us from God's love, and He continually seeks us out.

He Loves being with you

Luke 15:4-6 *"What man of you, having a hundred sheep, if he loses one of them, does not leave the ninety-nine in the wilderness, and go after the one which is lost until he finds it? [5] And when he has found it, he lays it on his shoulders, rejoicing. [6] And when he comes home, he calls together his friends and neighbours, saying to them, 'Rejoice with me, for I have found my sheep which was lost!'*

In ***Luke 15:4-6***, Jesus shared the parable of the lost sheep, revealing the shepherd's heart: despite having 99 with Him, He longs to find the one missing. He leaves the 99 to find me, to find you.

Sometimes we may wonder, 'Jesus has many faithful followers; I am not good enough, not faithful like them. Maybe Jesus is tired of me?' No, Jesus has many, but He still longs for you, always.

God's unwavering presence is a beacon of hope in the

darkest of times. Even when we stumble and fall, He remains steadfast, refusing to abandon us. The story of Judas' betrayal is a poignant reminder of this truth. It was not Jesus who released Judas from His grasp, but rather Judas who chose to let go. And yet, had Judas returned to Jesus, seeking forgiveness and mercy, I believe that Jesus would have forgiven him.

This is the same love that Jesus illustrated in the parable of the prodigal son in ***Luke 15:11-32***.

In the parable, the son, fueled by rebellion and a desire for independence, chose to leave his father's loving presence. But when he finally came to his senses and returned home, his father's response was not one of rejection or anger, but rather of unbridled joy and affection. The father's arms were open wide, ready to envelop his son in a warm and loving embrace. This, too, is the heart of our heavenly Father, who longs to welcome us back home, no matter how far we may have wandered.

He loves being with you, being with me, even at our worst (**Romans 5:8**). He loves us unconditionally. ***Jeremiah 31:3*** *"Yes, I have loved you with an everlasting love; Therefore with lovingkindness I have drawn you.* This understanding has deepened my relationship with God, shifting my focus from fleeting experiences to eternal promises. I have learned to trust His presence, even when I do not feel it. I have discovered the beauty of His constant companionship, the peace that surpasses understanding. God's presence is my daily bread, my source of strength.

CHAPTER SIX

BEYOND PHYSICAL MANIFESTATIONS

It was a morning unlike any other, a moment in time I can still feel in the depths of my soul. In a small rented house, tucked away in the quiet of my tiny room, where a deep light shone amidst the stillness and shadows. The dawn had just broken, and as I awoke, I found myself lying on my bed, wrapped in the simplicity of the moment. But as soon as my eyes opened, an unmistakable feeling swept over me—a profound sense that someone had been waiting for me to wake up. It was not just a fleeting emotion or passing thought; it was a deep, unshakable conviction that there was a presence, waiting for me to open my eyes. And I knew with certainty that it was the Lord, waiting for me to wake up. As I opened my eyes, a wave of peace and warmth flooded my heart, and in that sacred moment, I felt so deeply loved, as though the Creator Himself had been holding space for me, patiently waiting for our communion. It was a love so pure and overwhelming, reminding me that no matter how small or unnoticed my life might seem, I was cherished beyond measure.

As I continue on my journey with God, His presence has become an increasingly precious and beautiful thing, a treasure that I cherish more and more with each passing day. His presence has become my daily need, it has become more beautiful than I ever could have imagined. It's as if my heart has been awakened to a new reality, one where every moment is infused with the possibility of encountering Him.

But, I have to admit, I used to think that His presence was only something I could feel during prayer and worship. I thought that it was only in those special moments, when I was intentionally seeking Him, that I could experience His presence. I would prepare my heart, quiet my mind, and focus on His words, hoping to catch a glimpse of His glory. And, yes, those moments were precious, and I treasured them deeply.

But, as I have grown closer to Him, I have come to realize that His presence is so much more than that. It's not just something I experience in church or during my quiet time. It's not just a feeling that comes and goes. His presence is a reality that surrounds me every moment of every day. It's the air I breathe, the ground I stand on, the rhythm of my heartbeat.

One day, I said to the Lord, 'Lord, I want to live a life where You will be with me and I will be with You all day. Do not give me a life where I will have to stay inside four walls, dealing with people.' Indirectly, I was saying Lord, I do not want to do a government office job, because at the time, I believed that having a job would prevent me from sitting in His presence for most of the day, as I thought His presence was only experienced during prayer and worship.

The physical manifestations of God's presence are glorious– undeniable displays of His power and love. I have been blessed to experience numerous moments of divine intervention, unforgettable encounters that have deepened my faith. Yet, I have also learned that confining God solely to these experiences can limit our understanding of His nature.

During my walk with the Lord, I have faced days when God seems silent, and I couldn't feel His presence. Those moments were excruciating, filled with uncertainty and doubt. I pleaded with the Lord, crying out for His response, but the silence persisted.

Doubts crept in, making me wonder if the Lord was still with me. Had He forsaken me? Was I unworthy of His presence? The thoughts swirled, threatening to undermine my faith.

But then, in the midst of my turmoil, the Lord spoke directly to my heart: 'I am with you always, whether you feel Me or not. I am as close to you when you don't feel Me as when you do.

These words, though simple, held profound truth. God's presence is not dependent on my emotions or experiences. He is not limited to moments of tangible manifestation.

Jesus promised His disciples, *'And surely I am with you always, to the very end of the age'* ***(Matthew 28:20)***. This assurance isn't based on feelings but on the unwavering character of God.

David, in **Psalm 23:4,** *declared, 'Even though I walk through the darkest valley, I will fear no evil, for you are with me; your rod and your staff comfort me.' David's confidence rested on God's presence, regardless of circumstances.*

Similarly, the apostle Paul wrote, *'For I am convinced that neither death nor life, neither angels nor demons, neither the present nor the future, nor any powers, neither height nor depth, nor anything else in all creation, will be able to separate us from the love of God that is in Christ Jesus our Lord'* ***(Romans 8:38-39)***.

God's presence transcends emotions and experiences. He is always with us, guiding, comforting, and empowering. May our faith be rooted in this unshakeable truth, trusting Him even in the silence.

In ***John 1:48***, we encounter a profound moment between Jesus and Nathanael. Though Nathanael had never met Jesus of Nazareth and knew nothing of Him, Jesus was already watching over him. In that quiet, unseen way, Jesus was present in Nathanael's life, even before he recognized Him. When Jesus spoke to Nathanael, revealing His divine insight, Nathanael was astonished. Jesus then reassured him, revealing a deeper truth—that He had always known him, even before they had met. This moment beautifully illustrates how, even in our ignorance, the Lord is always with us, watching, guiding, and knowing us more intimately than we realize.

Psalms 139:1-3 *O Lord, You have searched me and known me. You know my sitting down and my rising up; You understand my thought afar off. You comprehend my path and my lying down, And are acquainted with all my ways.*

God desires us to recognize His presence beyond emotions and experiences, grounding our faith in His unwavering Word. This steadfast trust empowers us to stand firm amidst life's challenges.

In the stillness or turmoil, God remains with us, unchanging and faithful. His presence is not dependent on our feelings but on His unshakeable promises.

As we navigate life's uncertainties, let's anchor our hearts in the living Word, embracing God's presence beyond fleeting emotions.

Do not misunderstand me; I earnestly desire every person to experience the Lord's glorious presence daily. I too crave such encounters and have been blessed with them. However, my faith is not dependent on feelings or experiences. I hold onto the truth that God remains as close to me when I do not feel Him as when I do.

As David exclaimed in ***Psalm 27:4***, *"One thing I have desired of the Lord, that will I seek: that I may dwell in the house of the Lord all the days of my life..." In Old Testament times, people had to physically enter the house of the Lord or a particular time or place. But through the grace of the Lord Jesus Christ, our bodies are now the temple (house) of the Lord* ***(1***

Corinthians 3:16: *"Do you not know that you are the temple of God and that the Spirit of God dwells in you?).*

We can live out David's desire daily. Yes, it's possible to abide in the Lord's presence all the days of our life.

Sadly, the devil deceives many believers, making them feel God is distant, despite biblical assurances. They know the Bible says God is with us, yet it becomes hard for them to believe it because they didn't feel it.

CHAPTER SEVEN

FAITH BEYOND FEELINGS

It's truly wonderful to experience God's presence and His tangible presence in our lives. I deeply long to have such encounters every day, as they ignite my faith and intensify my desire to be with Him always.

However, it's crucial to recognize that our faith and trust in God must transcend beyond our experiences and feelings. While experiences can strengthen our connection, our trust should remain unwavering, regardless of emotions.

It's glorious to experience God's presence, but our faith should be just as strong when we feel Him as when we don't. This understanding fosters a deeper relationship, built on trust rather than emotions.

Sometimes, even when you do not feel God's presence, remember and know that He is still with you. His presence is not dependent on our feelings but on His promise to never leave or forsake us ***(Hebrews 13:5)*** *Let your conduct be without covetousness; be content with such things as you* *have. For He Himself has said, "I will never leave you nor forsake you.*

One day, I was having time with my friends who do not believe in Jesus at my home. We were sharing laughter and conversation over tea and Maggi. As our discussion unfolded, Jesus became the topic of conversation.

Seizing the opportunity, I shared about Jesus and His transformative power. After sharing, I invited my friends to pray with me, and to my surprise, they agreed.

At that moment, I did not feel God's presence, but I prayed for my friends anyway. Remarkably, one of them exclaimed, "I feel like someone was here among us!" Instantly, I knew it was the Lord.

Confidently, I replied, "That's Jesus!" This experience taught me a profound truth: even when I don't feel Him, God is always with me (***Matthew 28:20***).

This realisation struck a chord deep within me:

- God's presence is not dependent on my emotions
- Prayer invites His tangible presence (***Acts 2:1-4)***
- Sharing Jesus can open doors to divine encounters

That day, my friends caught a glimpse of God's love, and I gained a deeper understanding of His unwavering presence in my life – with friends, family, or alone. God's presence manifested in your life, even when you did not feel Him.

Another similar remarkable encounter occurred during our outreach program in the city. Our youth group divided into teams to share the Gospel in streets and homes. My team and I visited a house where a young girl answered the door. We shared the Gospel with her and prayed together. Astonishingly, she revealed that while we prayed, she felt someone standing close to her. What's more remarkable is that she was not a Christian; she was a Buddhist. Yet, she experienced God's presence! We confidently told her, 'That was Jesus standing near you!' This experience reinforced a profound truth:

When you walk with the Lord, carrying His presence, those around you can experience God's presence through you, even if they do not believe in Him.

Once my pastor said, "*When you Sit in God's Presence, Your presence becomes a Ministry.*"
-Pastor Shajet Thomas

This encounter strengthened my faith and highlighted the power of:

- Sharing the Gospel
- Prayer
- Carrying God's presence

That day, we witnessed God's love transcending religious boundaries, touching hearts and minds.

Walk With Faith

Our walk with Christ is not dictated by feelings but by

faith in His words. Apostle Paul said our walk with the Lord is by faith ***(2 Corinthians 5:7** For we walk by faith, not by sight* ***)*** This unwavering trust empowers us to stand firm, even when emotions fluctuate.

Do not misunderstand - I am not suggesting you stop desiring to experience Him. On the contrary, I want you to know that the Lord is with you even when you don't feel Him. His presence transcends emotions and circumstances.

Experiencing His presence is one of the most precious and marvelous things you can have in your life as a Christian. In fact, I always ask the Lord, 'How can I experience You all the days of my life?' Because His presence is so wonderful, so real, and so marvellous.

The Bible affirms this longing in ***Psalm 34:8***, *'Oh, taste and see that the Lord is good.'* When I first tasted the presence of God, I was so desperate to tell people about His presence. It's a life-changing experience that I want everyone to have.

David's words in ***Psalm 63:1-2*** resonate deeply: *'You, God, are my God, earnestly I seek you; I thirst for you, my whole being longs for you, in a dry and parched land where there is no water.'*

I still remember the day when I experienced the tangible presence of God for the first time in my life and ministry. It was during Pastor Shajet's Zoom meeting, I was very new to this spiritual things, I was in my rented house joining the Zoom service.

During the service as our Pastor was praying for all he declared, 'Now the Lord wants to touch some of you.' In that instant, I felt an overwhelming desire to receive God's touch. I quickly lifted my hands, and said, 'Lord, it's me! Please touch me today anyhow I want to experience you!'

And then, it happened! Suddenly my hands began moving uncontrollably, waving like a fan. The sensation was uncontainable, a manifestation of God's presence coursing through me. Time stood still as I basked in this divine encounter.

The Zoom service ended, but I remained immersed in the overwhelming wave of God's presence. Tears of joy streamed down my face, mingling with sweat. My heart raced with excitement.

Overjoyed and still in awe, I rushed to share this experience with my mom. I told 'Mom, the Lord has touched me!' I exclaimed, hardly able to contain my emotions. 'My hands moved uncontrollably! I experienced the Lord today!'"

Experiencing God's presence physically and tangibly is a great privilege and glorious thing. Yet, what I want you to know today is that even without a physical or tangible touch, you can still experience His presence.

You cannot always have the physical vibrations or tangible presence, as you go about your daily life - work, classes, office, business, or duty. Imagine being in class and your body starts vibrating or shaking; the whole class would be scared and run away! The Lord will not do that.

But here is the amazing part: even without physical touch, you can still experience His marvellous presence. You can still hear the voice of the Holy Spirit in the midst of the market, amidst the chaos and noise.

God's presence transcends physical sensations. He's always with you, guiding and speaking to you, even in the most unexpected places.

I have often travelled to my childhood town, Khonsa, for ministry and returned to Itanagar. Many times, while returning to my present town, Itanagar, I came crying inside the bus and car.

One day, I was returning to Itanagar by bus, with many people inside, and an unknown person sitting near me. Then, on the way, I was meditating about the Lord and His goodness inside, and I started experiencing His presence, though it was not the physical vibration or power.

I could not hold my tears there. The person sitting near me might have thought I had gone through a breakup or someone broke my heart, that's why I am crying. I was like, 'People are seeing me, what will they think?' Yet, I couldn't hold my tears.

The same thing happened another time inside the car while returning from my hometown. I was in the car,

Bollywood songs were playing, they were talking inside the car, and I was crying in the back corner.

It happened many times to me. That day, I realised we can experience Him anytime, anywhere on this earth. Beyond the physical touch, we can experience Him with us.

In those moments, ***Psalm 139:7-10*** *came alive: Where can I go from Your Spirit? Or where can I flee from Your presence? [8] If I ascend into heaven, You are there; If I make my bed in hell, behold, You are there. [9] If I take the wings of the morning, And dwell in the uttermost parts of the sea, [10] Even there Your hand shall lead me, And Your right hand shall hold me.*

God's presence is not limited to physical sensations or specific locations. He is always with you, guiding, comforting, and empowering you.

When I say God's presence goes beyond physical sensations and shaking hands, I am not discouraging you from seeking those experiences. In fact, the physical manifestations of His presence are glorious, and you should desire them more each day. These experiences are a gift from God, a tangible expression of His love and presence in our lives.

In the Bible both in the old & new testament many people witnessed the mighty tangible and visible manifestation of God's presence.

Physical manifestations as in ***1 Kings 19:11-12*** *Then He* *said, "Go out, and stand on the mountain before the Lord." And behold, the Lord passed by, and a great and strong wind tore into the mountains and broke the rocks in pieces before the Lord, but the Lord was not in the wind; and after the wind an earthquake, but the Lord was not in the earthquake; [12] and after the earthquake a fire, but the Lord was not in the fire; and after the fire a still small voice.*

Exodus 33:11 *So the Lord spoke to Moses face to face, as a man speaks to his friend. And he would return to the camp, but his servant Joshua the son of Nun, a young man, did not depart from the tabernacle.*

Acts 9:3-5 *As he journeyed he came near Damascus, and suddenly a light shone around him from heaven. [4] Then he fell to the ground, and heard a voice saying to him, "Saul, Saul, why are you persecuting Me?" [5] And he said, "Who are You, Lord?" Then the Lord said, "I am Jesus, whom you are persecuting. It is hard for you to kick against the goads."*

Acts 2:2-3 *And suddenly there came a sound from heaven, as of a rushing mighty wind, and it filled the whole house where they were sitting. [3] Then there appeared to them divided tongues, as of fire, and one sat upon each of them.*

There are many encounters in the Bible both in the new and old testament, which means the manifestation of God's presence is real.

However, we must remember that God's presence transcends physical sensations. It's essential to cultivate a deep, inner connection with Him through prayer, worship, and scripture.

In ***2 Corinthians 5:7***, *Paul writes, 'For we live by faith, not by sight.'* While physical experiences can strengthen our faith, they shouldn't replace our trust in God's character.

Desire both the physical and spiritual manifestations of God's presence. Seek His tangible expressions of love, but also nurture a deep, inner connection with Him.

By embracing both aspects, you will experience a more profound, intimate relationship with God, one that transforms your life and empowers you to share His love with others.

Having a deep understanding of His Word will actually increase your longing for these experiences. As you delve into Scripture, you'll discover the depth of God's character, His faithfulness, and His desire to commune with us. This understanding will fuel your desire for more encounters with Him, more moments of His tangible presence.

Through this book, I wish to gently remind or encourage you in two important ways:

1. If you have not yet encountered the presence of God in your life, or if you struggle to believe, I want to assure you that His presence is undeniably real. You can experience Him(Jesus), in a way that will transform your heart and life.

2. And if you have already tasted His glorious presence,

I want to encourage you to remember that His presence is far beyond the scope of any single experience. It is not limited to moments or feelings; it is a constant, boundless reality that extends beyond our understanding.

In my journey with the Lord, I have encountered people who love the Lord and are very faithful in serving Him, yet seem to miss out on personal encounters that could profoundly impact their walk with Him. And some people have experienced the manifestations of His presence but limit him to their experiences. This highlights a crucial misunderstanding: God's presence extends far beyond our experiences.

We often prioritise encounters and feelings over the unwavering foundation of faith – the Word of God. While experiences can be transformative, they should not replace our trust in God's character.

The Word of God serves as our anchor, providing unshakeable assurance of His presence. ***Hebrews 11:1*** *"Now faith is the substance of things hoped for, the evidence of things not seen."* It defines faith as 'confidence in what we hope for and assurance about what we do not see.' Our faith should not hinge on fleeting emotions or intermittent experiences.

Consider the biblical accounts of David, who, despite facing immense challenges, declared, *'I have set the Lord always before me. Because he is at my right hand, I will not be shaken'* ***(Psalm 16:8)***. David's faith rested on God's unchanging nature, not temporary experiences.

Similarly, the apostle Paul, who encountered the risen Christ (Acts 9), did not rely solely on that experience. He wrote, *'I know whom I have believed, and am convinced that he is able to guard what I have entrusted to him until that day'* ***(2 Timothy 1:12).***

Let's build our faith on the solid rock of God's Word, acknowledging His presence beyond our experiences. As we stand on this foundation, we'll find unwavering confidence in His love and companionship, even in times of doubt or uncertainty. ***Matthew 7:24*** *Therefore whoever hears these sayings of Mine, and does them, I will liken him to a wise man who built his house on the rock:*

CHAPTER EIGHT

TANGIBLE PRESENCE OF GOD

In the peaceful surroundings of Borum Village, near Naharlagun train station in Arunachal Pradesh, India, our church, Revival Blessing International Ministries (RBIM), has a special fasting program every second week of the month, we observe a three-day fast on Friday, Saturday, and Sunday.

Before the Borum our Church was located at Nirjuli D-sector 15 minutes away from our new Church location, Borum.

As always, we were having a three-day fast program at Nirjuli D-sector Harvest Church. After one of the services during the break, I was in my room worshipping the Lord. I said , Lord , I know you are here, Lord, I want to experience you.'

With my guitar, I began worshipping. Then, something extraordinary happened. My hands, holding the guitar chords, started vibrating intensely. The sensation was unlike anything I had experienced before. It felt like an unseen force was resonating through every part of me.

The vibration of His presence was so powerful that it seemed to expand the sides of my hands and fingers. The increase was extreme, as if my hands had grown larger. I couldn't maintain my grip on the chords.

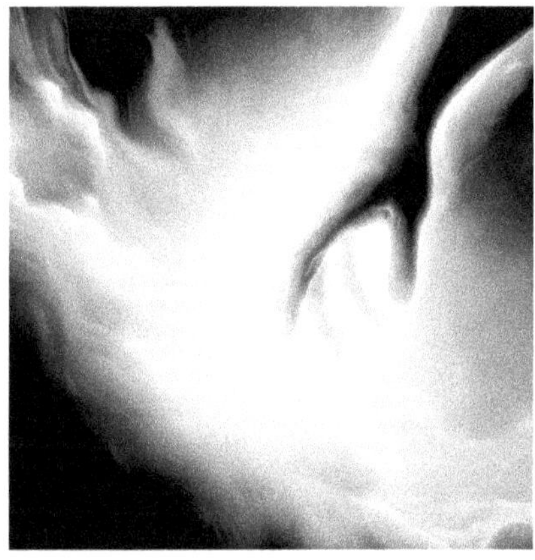

As I could not hold my hands on the guitar's fret, I kept aside the guitar and I lifted my hands. I distinctly felt someone grasping both hands. The sensation was incredibly real, making me open my eyes, expecting to see the physical hands of the Lord. Though they remained invisible. In that moment, the boundary between the spiritual and physical worlds seemed to fade. God's presence became almost visible to me.

This unforgettable encounter reinforced a profound truth: God desires to manifest His presence in our lives, bridging the spiritual and physical realms.

The Unexpected Moment

I have learned that it's often in the midst of our daily routines that God surprises us with His presence and His plans. It's in the ordinary moments, the ones we often take for granted, that He reveals Himself to us in unexpected ways. A conversation with a stranger, a chance encounter with a friend, a sudden insight or inspiration these are the moments when God breaks into our lives and reminds us that He is always at work, even when we're not aware of it.

That day began like any other. I was dropping my elder sister at the hospital for her duty. But little did I know, God had other plans.

As we reached the hospital, a sudden remembrance struck me - her personal quarters, provided by the hospital department, were empty. Without hesitation, I turned my scooty around and headed to her room. The stillness of the empty room beckoned me.

I entered, closing the door behind me, and fell to my knees. The quiet solitude was a sanctuary, inviting me to pour out my heart. I began singing songs and worshipping, knowing that the Lord was present with me.

The words of my songs became prayers, and my prayers became whispers of devotion. Moments later, I felt an unmistakable presence near me – the precious Holy Spirit.

Unlike previous experiences, this one was not marked by vibrations or shaking; but by a profound sense of the Holy Spirit's person. I knew that the Holy Spirit was in the room.

This presence was so glorious that I wanted to remain there forever. In that instant, I understood David's heartfelt cry in ***Psalm 27:4***.*"One thing I have desired of the Lord, That I will seek: That I may dwell in the house of the Lord All the days of my life, To behold the beauty of the Lord, And to inquire in His temple."*

Ironically, I had an important class to attend that day. Being in my final year of higher secondary school. One I could not afford to miss. Torn between staying in the room, basking in God's presence, and attending my class, I confessed to the Holy Spirit.

Lord, I do not want to leave this place," I pleaded, "knowing You desire to be here with me even more than I do. But I must attend my class today." The words felt like a betrayal.

Reluctantly, I rose from my knees, my heart heavy with the thought of leaving. With a deep breath, I departed, carrying the memory of that glorious encounter.

CHAPTER NINE

CONSCIOUSNESS OF HIS PRESENCE

The physical manifestations of God's presence—such as vibrations and shaking of hands and other experiences—are truly glorious. I long to experience it everyday. However, there is another profound level of experiencing His presence, one that transcends physical sensations. Sometimes, God's presence is just as real, even when we do not experience tangible signs.

In these moments, we can still experience the glorious companionship of His presence through the consciousness of His Word. This profound awareness of God's presence grows deeper as we meditate on Scripture, sensing His love, guidance, and peace.

While experiencing Him physically is wonderful, do not rely solely on feelings to acknowledge Him. Our faith must be rooted in His Word, His promises, and His character.

Remember, God's presence is not limited to physical sensations or emotions. He is always with us, guiding us, and empowering us to live for Him.

My brother once asked, "Brother Liam, with your busy ministry schedule - services, fellowships, programs, studies, and personal work - how do you find time to spend with the Lord?"

I replied, "As I am talking to you now, I know that the Lord is here. I am training my consciousness to acknowledge Him. While alone time with the Lord is precious, carrying His presence consciousness allows me to be with Him anywhere, anytime."

I deeply cherish private moments with the Lord, and I actively seek opportunities to be with Him alone. Jesus also valued alone time with His Father. Scripture reveals His frequent separations from His disciples to pray, as seen in ***Matthew 14:13,***

Luke 6:12 *Now it came to pass in those days that He went out to the mountain to pray, and continued all night in prayer to God.*

Mark 1:35 *Now in the morning, having risen a long while before daylight, He went out and departed to a solitary place; and there He prayed.*

Those moments alone with the Lord are truly beautiful and transformative.

However, I want to emphasise that being with Him should not be limited to personal, quiet times. While these moments are precious, our connection with God can transcend beyond them. We can maintain a living, breathing relationship with Him even amidst life's chaos.

Jesus, the Son of God, often separated Himself from the crowds to be alone with His Father. But His connection with God was not limited to those moments of solitude. Even when He was surrounded by people, teaching, healing, and performing miracles, Jesus was still fully connected with His Father. He was never disconnected from God's presence, whether He was alone in prayer or in the midst of a bustling crowd. Jesus said to his disciples when He was asked to show the father, He said, "if you have seen me you've seen the father." ***(John 14:9)***

His presence in our lives should not be limited to just our private moments or spaces. It is not a presence that only visits in moments of prayer or worship, It is meant to fill every moment of our day and every part of our life.

Amidst the busyness and distractions of life, it's easy to become consumed by the noise of the world around us. We often find ourselves distracted, caught up in the worries, tasks, and responsibilities that fill our days, leaving little room to recognize the quiet, constant presence of God. Yet, the truth is that His presence is always with us, surrounding us in every moment. The challenge lies not in the absence of God, but in our awareness of Him.

We do not lack His presence; we are not always conscious of it. This is why it becomes so vital to train our spirits and minds to become more attuned to His divine nearness. By cultivating a daily awareness, we invite His presence to guide and shape every moment, transforming our lives with

His love and peace.

We do not lack His presence; we are not just always aware of it. That is why it's crucial to train our consciousness to acknowledge His presence daily.

Meditate on His presence in the midst of the market, amidst the hustle and bustle. As you sit with family and friends, engage in conversations yet simultaneously train your consciousness to recognize God's presence. ***Psalms 16:8*** *AMP I have set the Lord continually before me; Because He is at my right hand, I will not be shaken.*

This awareness is not automatic; it's a process. The more you train your consciousness, the more sensitive it becomes to His presence.

By intentionally cultivating this awareness, you will:

- Develop a deeper sense of God's omnipresence
- Find strength in His constant companionship
- Live with greater purpose and joy

In the stillness and in the noise, through prayer, worship, and meditation, we can remain connected to God. His presence can be our constant companion, guiding us through life's challenges.

Yet, I urge you: never miss the chance to be with Him alone and desire for the encounters. Those moments refine your faith, rejuvenate your spirit, and deepen your intimacy with God. They equip you to face life's trials with courage, wisdom, and hope.

May we prioritise these sacred moments with God, embracing both the tranquillity and the turmoil as opportunities to cultivate an unshakeable connection with God.

CHAPTER TEN

PRESENCE FOREVER

Such knowledge is too wonderful for me; It is high, I cannot attain it. Where can I go from Your Spirit? Or where can I flee from Your presence? If I ascend into heaven, You are there; If I make my bed in hell, behold, You are there. If I take the wings of the morning, And dwell in the uttermost parts of the sea, Even there Your hand shall lead me, And Your right hand shall hold me. ***-Psalms 139:6-10***

As I share this with you, I want to leave an indelible mark on your heart: the presence of God is breathtakingly real. It's a truth that transcends human understanding, a reality that surpasses fleeting emotions and experiences.

Continue to yearn for encounters and manifestations of His presence, deeply rooted in unwavering faith in His words. Remember, His presence transcends physical sensations or emotional experiences. He is with you regardless of tangible manifestations.

Do not limit His presence to just feelings and

manifestations or extraordinary events. His presence permeates every moment, every breath. Know this: His presence never leaves you. It's constant, unwavering, and unrelenting.

Jesus promised, "*And surely I am with you always, to the very end of the age*" (***Matthew 28:20)***. This timeless assurance echoes through eternity, a constant reminder of His unwavering commitment.

In Hebrews 13:5, God declares, "Never will I leave you; never will I forsake you." This promise is not conditional; it's unconditional, unwavering, and unrelenting.

May this truth ignite an unquenchable thirst within you, fueling your desire for more of Him. May His presence be your guiding light, comforting embrace, and steadfast companion.

The more you desire for him the more He will reveal the beauty of his presence. Keep desiring his wonderful presence more and more everyday. Seek him in every part of your life, never miss any chance to know him more.

I want to encourage you to never lose your thirst for Him and His presence. Knowing that His presence goes beyond what you feel and experience will make your faith firmly strong. Yet, may you always yearn to experience Him more deeply.

Even if you have encountered Him many times, keep longing for Him. In fact, the more you experience Him, the more your thirst for Him will grow, you will be more passionate for Him.

Do not settle for past experiences; press on to know Him more. His presence is a wellspring of life, transforming and renewing you.

Embrace the beauty of His presence, and let it transform your life. As you walk in the awareness of His constant presence, may your heart overflow with joy, peace, and gratitude.

Let's cherish the beauty of God's presence, making it our highest priority.

Remember, the Lord wants you to be with him more than you want him to be with you. He is more willing to reveal himself to us more than we want to know him.

One day, I said to the Lord, 'Lord, never take away your presence from me, you can take away my breath but not your presence. There was a time in my life, the Lord was using me. People were appreciating me, yet deep down I knew those days I was not experiencing His presence for many days. Then I said to the Lord, 'Lord, I cannot live like this, it feels like something is missing in my life. I do not want the people's appreciation without your presence, even Lord, I do not want your anointing without your presence in my life, I do not want your gifts without your presence. I did not know whether this was right to pray or not but I was saying Lord, even if you take everything away from me, but never take away your presence from me. Lord, even if you take away all of your gifts from me do not take away your presence from me.'

That day I realised that I can no longer live without His presence in my life. *And felt the heart of David when he cried, "Do not cast me away from Your presence, And do not take Your Holy Spirit from me."*
Psalms 51:11

As I sought to deepen my understanding of God's presence, I reached out to my brethren, curious to know if they too had experienced the same profound sense of connection. I asked them, "What does His presence mean to you?" Their heartfelt responses touched my heart. They said:

"He makes me complete, without His presence my life does not have any existence." - Kathryn Debom Tamin

"The presence of God is the most important and precious thing that my Lord Jesus has given to me on this side of my spiritual walk till I see Him face to face." - Tubin Mudang

"The presence of God is the very essence of my spiritual journey. It makes me understand the direction to follow which leads to Christ my saviour." - Techi David

Then I understood, the Lord wants everyone to experience his wonderful presence and his precious relationship. The question is are we willing to open our hearts to Him.

Yes, if you want to experience Him in your life, the first thing you need to do is just to surrender yourself. He does not require you to pay any price; He just wants you to open your heart and fully surrender before Him.

If you are somebody who has never experienced the presence of God in your life, then today you can experience Him, because the Lord loves you. I truly believe this book did not come into your hands by mistake; it's the will of the Lord to call you to His marvelous presence.

Now, if you want to experience the things I shared, the first thing you have to do is just surrender yourself. Even right now, as you are reading this, you can surrender yourself and pray to the Lord, saying:

Lord, I know You are here with me. I am just here right now before You, Lord. I want to experience You, to know You more intimately, and to feel Your presence in my life. I surrender myself to You, Lord. Have Your way in me, and fill me with Your love and peace.

As you pray this prayer, remember that the Lord is faithful and just. He will hear your prayer. So, take a step of faith today, and surrender yourself to the Lord. He will meet you right where you are, and transform your life in ways you never thought possible.

Everyday I remind myself, let it be my heart's deepest longing and prayer to be a person who craves and loves the presence of God above all else. More than ministry, spiritual gifts, and power, may I love His presence. May I always yearn to be someone who values intimate moments with Him more than any earthly achievement or spiritual accomplishment.

May your times with God be sweet, transformative, and life-giving. May his presence become your breath

Psalms 73:28 *But it is good for me to draw near to God; I have put my trust in the Lord God, That I may declare all Your works.*

Psalms 16:11 *You will show me the path of life; In Your presence is fullness of joy; At Your right hand are pleasures forevermore.*

May God bless you.

Thank you for being a part of this journey with me. As we part ways, I want to leave you with a reminder that is dear to my heart: Jesus loves you! No matter who you are, where you come from, or what you have done, His love for you is unwavering and unconditional.

I want to assure you that His love is not based on your past or your performance, but on His own character and nature. He loves you because He is love, and He desires to have a personal relationship with you.

If you are someone who has not yet received Jesus Christ into your life, I want to invite you to consider making the most important decision you will ever make. Surrendering your life to Jesus will be the best decision you will ever make, and it's one that you will never regret.

I can confidently say this because I have experienced it for myself. If He can change my life, I know He can change yours too.

If you are ready to receive the Lord into your life, I want to guide you through a simple prayer. Please repeat after me:

Dear Heavenly Father,

I come to You in humility and repentance, acknowledging that I am a sinner in need of Your forgiveness and salvation.

I believe that Jesus Christ is Your Son, who died on the cross for my sins and rose again from the dead.

I confess my faith in Jesus Christ as my Lord and Savior, and I receive Him into my heart.

Please forgive me of my sins and wash me clean with the blood of Jesus.

I surrender my life to You, and I ask that You fill me with Your Holy Spirit, guiding me and empowering me to live a life that honours You.

Thank You for saving me and giving me eternal life.

In Jesus' name, I pray. Amen.

The grace of the Lord

Jesus Christ, and the love of God, and the communion of the Holy Spirit be with you all.

Amen.

-II Corinthians 13:14

Jesus Loves you!

www.ingramcontent.com/pod-product-compliance
Lightning Source LLC
LaVergne TN
LVHW070224170826
845679LV00033B/2184

9798896738503